BITCOIN

How to make 1400X in 5 years

Gary Bukowski

© Copyright 2017 - All rights reserved.

The contents of this book may not be reproduced, duplicated or transmitted without direct written permission from the author.

Under no circumstances will any legal responsibility or blame be held against the publisher for any reparation, damages, or monetary loss due to the information herein, either directly or indirectly.

Legal Notice:

This book is copyright protected. This is only for personal use. You cannot amend, distribute, sell, use, quote or paraphrase any part or the content within this book without the consent of the author.

Disclaimer Notice:

Please note the information contained within this document is for educational and entertainment purposes only. Every attempt has been made to provide accurate, up to date and reliable complete information. No warranties of any kind are expressed or implied. Readers acknowledge that the author is not engaging in the rendering of legal, financial, medical or professional advice. The content of this book has been derived from various sources. Please consult a licensed professional before attempting any techniques outlined in this book.

By reading this document, the reader agrees that under no circumstances are is the author responsible for any losses, direct or indirect, which are incurred as a result of the use of information contained within this document, including, but not limited to, —errors, omissions, or inaccuracies.

Also by the Author

Blockchain: A 60 minute guide to Blockchain Technology

Ethereum: How to make 36 times your money in 1 year

CONTENTS

Introduction ------- 1

Chapter 1: The Beginning ------- 3

   Pre-History ------- 4

   The Starting ------- 5

Chapter 2: History ------- 6

   Rise and fall! ------- 7

Chapter 3: Interesting Characters Involved ------- 12

   Satoshi Nakamoto ------- 12

   Winklevoss Twins ------- 13

   Hal Finney ------- 13

   Gavin Andreson ------- 14

   Andreas Antonopoulos ------- 15

   Roger Ver ------- 16

Chapter 4: Investing ------- 17

Chapter 5: Benefits ------- 22

   Financial Self-Determinism and Control ------- 22

   Irreversible Transactions ------- 22

   No Requirement for Middlemen ------- 24

   Lower Cost of Transactions ------- 27

   It Works Around the World ------- 28

   Inflationary Hedge for Long Term Savings or Investments ------- 28

Chapter 6: Risks ------------------------------- **30**

   Irreversible Transactions ---------------------- 30

   Potential Hacking Threats -------------------- 31

   Volatility of Bitcoin Prices --------------------- 32

   Anti-Inflationary ---------------------------------- 34

   Computational Attack --------------------------- 36

   Regulatory Ambiguity --------------------------- 38

   Risk of Loss --------------------------------------- 40

Chapter 7: Future ------------------------------- **41**

Conclusion --------------------------------------- **43**

Bibliography/Reference ------------------------ **45**

Introduction

You know, I have to be sincerely honest with you. This book was the result of a couple months of research and hard work and I really want to THANK YOU for deciding to read it. It means a lot to me and I hope you enjoy reading it as much as I enjoyed writing it.

This book tells you the story about how a digital currency turned into one of the most valuable inventions of the 21st century.

Bitcoin is now a strong currency that is used by millions of users around the world. Some naysayers worry about all the secrecy behind the currency, but people continue using it because they want a currency that is free from governmental intervention. Some are even calling it a democratic form of currency that can be officially used for all transactions.

But, the most interesting part about Bitcoin is not its system and the money you can make from it. All of that is, of course, essential; you will learn all about it in this book, but the part that will intrigue anyone is how Bitcoin was created and how that knowledge can be used to better your financial position.

Bitcoin came to the mainstream from online forums and crowd invention. The concept was first brought to the Internet by the great inventor, Satoshi Nakamoto (an amusing person whose identity is still a secret) and then was slowly developed with the influence of many websites, tech gurus and investors.

Various people got involved from the very beginning, and it is interesting to see how Bitcoin slowly evolved with the help of these people to become the greatest CryptoCurrency of our time. Many people have made millions of dollars by getting involved with the Bitcoin business from its inception, but it has also led to massive losses for many.

So, if you want to know the suspicious yet fascinating story of Bitcoin and how you can use it to make money, then this is the book for you.

Chapter 1

The Beginning

Rumors of Bitcoin first started circulating in online chat rooms in 2008. It began when Satoshi Nakamoto contacted Hal Finney, a computer programmer about an online electronic currency that is generated or 'mined' over the Internet at a fixed rate. It is not controlled or tracked by any governmental or non-governmental organizations.

Every time a Bitcoin is mined, it is stored on a general ledger. However, this ledger does not reveal whom the Bitcoin belongs to.

Hal Finney was given access to a program that 'mined' these Bitcoins. 'Mining' requires a complicated online mathematical problem to be solved using a solution comprising 64 digits. Once a problem is solved, a Bitcoin is created, and the miner receives these Bitcoins. Bitcoins are encrypted using cryptography to provide privacy.

Bitcoin users have a virtual address, effectively a string of 27-34 letters and numbers, where Bitcoins are sent. There is no register of these addresses, meaning that they offer anonymity to the owner. These virtual addresses are stored in Bitcoin wallets. The only risk is that if the underlying data is lost then so are the Bitcoins.

Given the lack of a trail and the absence of government monitoring, online communities were initially very excited about the potential benefits Bitcoin offered to help societies that were underserved by the government.

While Bitcoin was an exciting concept, there were several attempts to create digital currencies by different programmers who were free from government intervention. However, all of these currencies had failed, and it was only Bitcoin that seemed to work as an online digital currency used for carrying out transactions.

The next section will talk about the various things that were happening when Bitcoin was created and its early days.

Pre-History

It's important to know about the people who were involved with the whole digital currency thing even before Bitcoin came out.

Three guys, Vladimir Oksman, Neal Kin and Charles Bry, filed a claim for an encryption patent. This happened just a few days before the first traces of Bitcoin came to light. In the same month, these three went ahead and registered a site named Bitcoin.org with the help of a server, which allowed people to create websites anonymously.

The three have denied any link to being the creators of Bitcoin or even being involved in the process, but people continue to think that all three of them together used the pseudonym, Satoshi Nakamoto.

At the same time, many other digital currencies were being developed. None of them were even remotely successful and were far from the sophistication that was used to build the Bitcoin network. Ecash – an issuer-based protocol that was developed by David Chaum, Hashcash, which was a proof-of-work scheme used for spam control designed by Stefan Brands and Adam Back, b-money – the first digital scarcity based CryptoCurrency made by Wei Dai and many others. These inventions are essential because they influenced the way Bitcoin worked and in many cases, complimented its functioning.

The Starting

The first time Bitcoin was ever mentioned was in a paper by Satoshi Nakamoto titled: "Bitcoin: A Peer-to-Peer Electronic Cash System."

In this article, he revealed his idea for a new invention that would change the world of finance. The article went into extreme details to talk about how Bitcoin works, the problem of pirating and how Bitcoin can gain legitimacy.

This led to the mining of the first Bitcoin block called the 'genesis block' that was owned by Satoshi. The genesis block at this point is valued at a total of US $2.8 billion. The Bitcoins in Satoshi's wallet have never been spent, and the entry can still be seen in the transaction log.

Chapter 2

History

Bitcoin first received value in normal currency from the New Liberty Standard, and it was established that the value of a Bitcoin at $1 is 1,309 BTC. Funnily enough, the equation was used to calculate this and took into account the cost of electricity that was utilized by the computer that created the Bitcoin.

Post the financial crisis; Bitcoin began to gain increasing credibility, especially since no government could control it. However, there was a fault: some users had identified a way to access other people's Bitcoins and spend it.

Organizations such as WikiLeaks were keen to use Bitcoins due to the anonymity it provided them; however, Nakamoto was not comfortable with this and was worried that associating with controversial organizations such as WikiLeaks would give Bitcoin a negative reputation.

Nakamoto actively retreated from online communities who were exploring Bitcoin's various uses because of the concerns they had around using Bitcoin for unethical initiatives.

On 22nd May 2010 Bitcoin achieved a new milestone when it was indirectly used to buy pizza. Bitcoin forums continue to celebrate this day till today by calling it the Bitcoin Pizza Day. On this day Laszlo Hanyecz, a programmer who was using the Bitcoin Talk forum paid another user 10,000 BTC for two pizzas from Papa John's. The technology was relatively new at that time and this cost Hanyecz $25 back then, but now the value of those Bitcoins is $5.12 million. It is widely considered as the first commercial transaction that took place with Bitcoin as the medium. Satoshi himself conducted the actual first transaction when he sent Bitcoins to Hal Finney.

Rise and fall!

In July 2010, Mt. Gox, a Bitcoin exchange based in Japan, was launched by software programmer Jed McCaleb, who saw the need for an exchange that traded both Bitcoins and currencies. He sold Mt. Gox to developer Mark Karpeles, as he did not have the capacity to grow the exchange to its full potential.

By April 2013, 70% of the world's Bitcoin trades were being processed through Mt. Gox. Mt. Gox had to suspend trading due to an increased demand for Bitcoins and the respective price surge in Bitcoins to stabilize its value.

By the end of 2013, Mt. Gox was scaling swiftly and was unable to meet client demands for withdrawal requests to exchange Bitcoins into dollars, resulting in severe regulatory issues with the US authorities.

In early 2014, all withdrawals were paused due to a bug that disguised Bitcoin transactions. Accordingly, it appeared that many transactions had not been made when in fact they had. Eventually, trading was suspended and Mt. Gox applied for bankruptcy protection in the US and sought liquidation rights in Tokyo.

Bitcoin, however, was put on the map when it was used as the only currency for making transactions on an online website called 'Silk Road.' Silk Road was an online black marketplace that traded in illegal goods such as drugs. Bitcoin was the perfect currency for the trading platform, as it enabled the buyer and the seller to remain anonymous. Its users grew rapidly and ironically ended up drawing attention worldwide, despite the intentions of its founder, Ross Ulbricht, to maintain a low profile.

Silk Road was shut down in October 2013 as a result of an FBI investigation. In November 2013 a second version of the site was launched, and it too was shut down. Ulbricht was convicted of participating in a criminal venture and facilitating illegal drugs on the dark net along with six other charges resulting in a life sentence in a Manhattan prison.

Funnily enough, this made the FBI the owner of the second largest Bitcoin wallet in the world. The largest wallet still belongs to the finder Satoshi Nakamoto, but the FBI still has more Bitcoins than people like the Winklevoss twins who say that they have cornered about 1% of all Bitcoins.

BitInstant, another Bitcoin exchange, was also shut down as a result of Silk Road closing down. BitInstant launched in 2011. Its founders Gareth Nelson and Charlie Shrem wanted to create an exchange where users could purchase Bitcoins in different retail stores such as Walmart.

In 2013, due to a boom in demand for Bitcoin (the Bitcoin price had tripled), the number of transactions being processed by BitInstant users grew significantly, and BitInstant struggled to meet demand. The Winklevoss brothers invested $1.5m to allow the exchange to hire more staff and improve its software to meet demand. (The Winklevoss brothers themselves had bought 1% of all the Bitcoins in circulation during Bitcoin's early years and had launched an exchange-traded Bitcoin investment fund.)

In July 2013, BitInstant had to suspend its services due to a lack of liquidity. Sadly BitInstant's users were not impressed. They could not liquidate their Bitcoins and lodged approximately 17,000 complaints. A lawsuit was filed against the company.

In early 2014, CEO Charlie Shrem was convicted of money laundering on the grounds that he had sold $1 million Bitcoins to Silk Road users. This was the final nail in the coffin for BitInstant.

BitInstant's other major investor, Wences Casares, an Argentine Fintech entrepreneur was a huge believer in Bitcoin, stating that it would be bigger than the Internet.

Casares family faced huge financial losses in Argentina due to deflation and devaluation of the Argentine Peso, and he felt that Bitcoin offered a solution to the volatile and incoherent nature of traditional currencies.

When Casares initially purchased Bitcoins, there was nowhere to store them. Accordingly, he created a vault comprising global servers where these could be stored. The servers were highly secure, had biometric access and were constantly filmed. The Meridian Insurance Group also insured the vault. Other Bitcoin enthusiasts and friends were interested in Casares vaults as a potential solution to their storage dilemmas. Accordingly, Casares founded Xapo, a startup that offered a Bitcoin 'wallet', essentially comprising the vaults that he had created.

More recently, there has been an increasing demand from China for Bitcoins to overcome the ban on Chinese money leaving the country, and the currency has hit a $1,000 high. The Renminbi has fallen 7% hinting at a potential negative correlation between the two currencies. With more and more people disillusioned by local currency and the control governments have over them, Bitcoin is starting to look like a very viable alternative, with some treating the currency as a haven asset.

The currency also increased in value due to the 2016 demonetization of high-value notes in India and the capital controls imposed in Venezuela.

Chapter 3

Interesting Characters Involved

Bitcoin has turned into one the world's best investment opportunity as more and more people make money by buying and trading it. This chapter will tell you about the various people that got involved in the creation of Bitcoin and those who made money from it.

Satoshi Nakamoto

The creator of Bitcoin is considered to be a Japanese national, but nobody can know for sure. He disappeared from the online forums about six years ago and hasn't been heard from since. For all we know, he could be a man, woman or a group of people.

There have been speculations to determine his identity, but nobody has owned up to it yet. Some people researched into everything that Satoshi did before he disappeared to find out who exactly he is. This includes making activity charts to determine what area he lived in. People even figured out that because his activity was very low during certain hours, it meant that he slept during this time and on that basis, it was concluded that he must have lived in the Greenwich Time zone.

Even if people continue to think that it's the CIA behind the Bitcoin, it cannot be denied that whoever created it was a genius and that it is still a currency that allows people to not deal with government regulation. His Bitcoin net worth is $2.8 Billion.

Winklevoss Twins

Tyler and Cameron Winklevoss are famous for their role in the development of Facebook. While they were economics students at Harvard, they hired Mark Zuckerberg to build a social media website. They later found out that he had developed Facebook behind their back and in a subsequent lawsuit they won $95 million.

The two twins then went on to invest in Bitcoin. They see Bitcoin as more valuable than gold, and they have currently cornered the market on Bitcoin by owning 1% of all Bitcoins. They launched Gemini in 2015; it's a Bitcoin exchange that allows people to buy, sell and trade in Bitcoin safely. Their collective Bitcoin net worth is $11 million.

Hal Finney

Hal Finney was one of the earliest people to get into the Bitcoin game, and he is also a well-known cryptographic activist. Finney was working on digital currency technologies even before Bitcoin came to light. He created the first reusable proof-of-work system. He was the first person to be part of a Bitcoin transaction back in 2009. He received Bitcoins that were sent by Satoshi Nakamoto.

He died in 2014 but before that he continued to work on experimental software called bcflick; this software used something called Trusted Computing, which helped in increasing the security of Bitcoin wallets. The Bitcoins that he had mined were spent on his medical bills to cure the disease that he had.

Gavin Andreson

A prominent and vocal member of the Bitcoin community, Gavin Andreson has worked directly with Satoshi Nakamoto. He collaborated with him to develop new source codes. He even has an alert key – this allows him to send messages to all Bitcoin clients if there is any major network problem. Before Satoshi vanished from the Internet, he handed over the source code repository and the alert key to him.

"Bitcoin is designed to bring us back to a decentralized currency of the people. This is like better gold than gold," explained Andreson back in 2011 to Forbes, when Bitcoin was still pretty new.

Andresen also left Bitcoin in April 2014, and now he focuses on larger issues. He still works as the Chief Scientist of the Bitcoin Foundation, but he is not the lead developer of Bitcoin anymore. His foundation tries to promote the use of Bitcoin around the world and works on standardizing it. He has also been critical of the new Bitcoin software and continues to support the use of Bitcoin classic.

Bitcoins also made him a millionaire, as he now owns Bitcoins worth US $2 million.

Andreas Antonopoulos

Andreas is a public speaker and a technology expert who works on making the Bitcoin technology easier to understand. He has become famous speaking in front of large audiences around the globe, explaining complex inventions like CryptoCurrency and Bitcoin.

He was one of the first people to explain the significance of Bitcoin as a free currency. He talked about how Bitcoin is free from any government and bank intervention that makes it a currency that only benefits the people and can't be influenced to help others. His aim is to assist people in understanding Bitcoin and get them connected to the global economy with its help.

He even wrote a book called Mastering Bitcoin, in which he explains the technicalities behind Bitcoin. He called Bitcoin the "internet of money" back in 2013 and has continued to fund open-source projects to develop Bitcoin.

Roger Ver

He was the first person to recognize the potential of Bitcoin and started investing in Bitcoin-related startups. He helped the first Bitcoin businesses to get seed funding by himself and has since worked on making Bitcoin more accessible. He is also known as the "Bitcoin Jesus" and is a proponent of the cause of voluntarism; the theory that all human interactions should be voluntary.

His company, Moneydealers, became one of the first mainstream sites to start accepting Bitcoin as currency. He also launched Bitcoinstore.com, the first site ever to accept Bitcoin for payment.

The current value of the Bitcoins he owns is $52 million.

Chapter 4

Investing

Investing in Bitcoin is a good idea right now, even though the value of Bitcoin fluctuates a lot – it's still a sound investment that will earn you a lot of money. If you want to invest in Bitcoin, you first have to learn how to acquire it.

Just like any currency works, you have to create Bitcoins if you want to make them work. But, you don't need an entity like the government to make money for everybody. Bitcoins are available for anyone to create and you can use them on your own. It's a positive that makes Bitcoin extremely unique and shows how evolved the field has become. It also ensures that a single entity can't monopolize the digital currency.

If you want to engage in a Bitcoin transaction, you will first need to get a Bitcoin address. This address will be like your bank account, and you will be able to store, send and receive Bitcoin units with it.

Instead of securing your Bitcoin units with the help of a vault, a public key setup is used to protect them. There is a particular code, which is used to make sure that the Bitcoin unit is in your name. This is what makes Bitcoins so charming for people who want to deal in

CryptoCurrency; transactions can't be traced, and it's impossible to steal them.

A Bitcoin address consists of two things – a public key, which anyone can view, and a private one, which the user is supposed to keep a secret. Anybody can send or transfer Bitcoin units to any public key, but you have to know the private key to transfer Bitcoin units or use them to buy goods and services.

Just because your Bitcoin address is available for the public to see, it doesn't mean that anyone can know that you are the owner of that Bitcoin address. This is why Bitcoins are referred to as "pseudonymous." The address can particularly be used as a means of listing information on what it is and to show that it is an authentic Bitcoin. The only key is that you will hold the rights to that particular Bitcoin if you have bought it, taken care of a transaction with it or have mined it yourself.

The protocols of Bitcoin use algorithms that are as powerful as the ones that are used by the National Security Agency/the NSA to encrypt all the secret level files and data. There is no limit to the number of Bitcoin addresses that you can create, and there's no charge either. Hence, it is possible for someone to create millions of Bitcoin addresses. This is what makes it impossible for anyone to copy someone's Bitcoin address and gain access to their Bitcoin funds. The expert Bitcoin users make several Bitcoin addresses for themselves, and they even protect these codes by storing them in a secured digital wallet.

Creating Bitcoins is a little complex because several steps are associated with it. The process is known as mining. A computer is used to 'mine' a proper chain, which is known as a block chain.

A program has to be used to mine a proper block chain; the program will use various codes to look for keys that can be used to register and create legal Bitcoins. How much time it takes for such a program to create a block can vary on a case-by-case basis. There are many sites and programs that you can use to mine Bitcoins on your own.

If a program can find and unlock a chain, then a Bitcoin will be created. This can be sent out in your name although you can also sell it to the highest bidder if you want.

If another person wants to transfer Bitcoins units to you, they'll have to use a program, which creates a transaction that has your Bitcoin address (the receiver) and the number of Bitcoin units that are being sent. To finalize the transaction, a cryptographic signature has to be input using his or her private key.

After the transaction has been submitted, it will be shown in a peer-to-peer Bitcoin network, which will validate the transaction by matching it with the sender's public key. The network will also check if the sender's Bitcoin address has sufficient units to carry out the transaction. When the initial verifications are complete, the transaction will be propagated to all of the other nodes in the Bitcoin network.

The final step for completely certifying a Bitcoin transaction is successfully adding it to a block in the Bitcoin blockchain. Currently, there are tens of thousands of independent computers that perform "mining" transactions in the Bitcoin network. Each of the computers collects the transactions that have been broadcasted by other nodes with the objective of guessing the number, which will solve a random cryptographic puzzle.

A chain will be designed to make a Bitcoin into what it is. A chain will consist of many key blocks to make it work right.

A block is a piece of data used in the process of getting a Bitcoin ready. It is kind of like a legal documentation of the qualities of the Bitcoin in question when you think about how it is generated.

The amazing part of the chain is that it can work with as many blocks as needed. As each of the blocks is discovered, the database of such blocks is appended into an ever-developing block chain. As of this writing, there are more than 150,000 available block chains in the whole Bitcoin network. All transactions that are part of the list encoded in the block chain are considered valid.

This security feature eradicates the likelihood that the Bitcoin units are spent twice as much. Think if it as if there is no real way how anyone can counterfeit Bitcoins. It makes for a safe transaction where you will get some currency and know that it can be used without worrying about whether or not it is functional.

Chapter 5

Benefits

What is it about Bitcoins that make them popular? Here's a look at why they are so advantageous today.

Financial Self-Determinism and Control

The Bitcoin network is one of a kind because it is the original digital storage of value where people can securely save Bitcoin units and enter into transactions without the need to rely on any third party regulatory body. After you have acquired and safely secured your Bitcoin units, it is almost impossible for other people (thieves, hackers, banks or even the government) to take them away from you. The government cannot authorize the freezing of your Bitcoin account nor stop you from entering into any transactions within the Bitcoin network.

Irreversible Transactions

Chargebacks are considered as one of the biggest problems of retail vendors. Almost all types of existing payment methods – credit cards, interbank transfers, and even PayPal – permit consumers to disprove any specific transactions so they can have their funds sent back to them. Vendors have no other choice but to go through a costly dispute process to gain back their money. There are even instances when the vendors will have to pay additional fees ranging from $ 10 to $ 50 for each chargeback transaction. A vendor can even be asked to pay extra penalty charges that can be as high as $ 25,000 if the regulatory institutions notice that they have an abnormally high rate of chargeback transactions.

A lot of online sellers have opted to shoulder a specific level of fraudulent chargeback transactions while spending more company funds on several security measures with the aim of detecting fraudulent transactions. In their effort to reduce their chargeback transactions, vendors normally require their customers to disclose certain personal information that is sometimes beyond what is considered essential to deliver the product or service purchased. This practice leads to the loss of privacy or confidentiality for the customers.

The Bitcoin network reverses this role of trust by making the Bitcoin transactions intrinsically irreversible. After a particular transaction has been validated and included in a block chain, it is no longer practical to have it reversed. It becomes the responsibility of the customer to trust the merchants that they will be entering transactions with.

Because there are a lot of ways to ascertain the integrity of a vendor including online ratings and word of mouth reputations, the "trust principle" of the Bitcoin system is a decently appropriate for online commerce. If we look at it, it a lot easier to verify the integrity of merchants compared to validate the integrity of all customers.

The fact that the Bitcoin can be tracked through the code used on an individual coin will help as well. It confirms the authenticity of the currency, so the people involved in a transaction will not be hesitant to take in the coin that you're trying to bring out.

Since a Bitcoin payment can no longer be reversed without the permission of the vendor, online vendors can now offer their products and services to a bigger market without requiring personal information from their consumers. The purpose is to create a semblance of security and safety for all people who want to get the most out of whatever they want to buy.

No Requirement for Middlemen

There are instances when the policies being implemented by payment processors are misaligned with the policies of those who receive the funds, such institutions who accept donations. One instance is when one blog owner, Helen Killer, requested donations from its followers that she intended to use to purchase Christmas gifts for children who come poor families. When Helen Killer was able to collect several thousands of dollars, her account with PayPal where the donations were sent was eventually frozen.

When she contacted a support representative of PayPal, Helen Killer was informed that her account was frozen because apparently, the "Donate" feature on PayPal can only be utilized by registered non-profit organizations. But PayPal later reversed this claim when they stated that any institution or individual could use the "Donate" feature of PayPal.

The original PayPal support representative that Killer talked to told her that her endeavor is "not a worthy cause, it's charity" and Killer will have to create a new website if she wanted to continue with her charitable cause and that presents could not be shipped to a distinct address from the consumer who transmitted money for them (which is basically irrational especially during a holiday season where a lot of people buy gifts to be delivered to another person).

When Helen Killer published her exasperating experience, she ultimately received an apology statement from the PayPal management who eventually ordered the unfreezing of her account. But for sure, there a lot of other stories from other frustrated PayPal users whose accounts have either been shut down or frozen for unreasonable reasons. Most probably, many of these frustrated users are not able to fight for their rights and they have just let go of their fund accounts altogether.

Another story to see comes from how much money you could lose through a middleman. Alex King, a software developer who creates open source software, had entirely ceased receiving donations from willing people when he realized that it costs him more money to receive the donations. In 2009, he noted that an unidentified user of his software donated $ 1 to his PayPal account. In his horror, he noted that $ 0.67 or 67% of the donation was deducted from his account for PayPal fees. Alex King decided to return the donation to the user.

He experienced another appalling situation when he saw that PayPal charged him $ 10 as chargeback fee, without giving him any prior notice. Alex King further shared that "I was never able to issue a refund to avoid this charge – the refund link was unavailable as the payment was listed as in dispute."

PayPal continues to expand its user base, but more and more online sellers notice that they are exposed to high risks of frozen accounts and chargeback fees. Bitcoin users are not exposed to the same risks primarily because Bitcoin transactions are considered irrevocable and can be received without the need for a middleman.

Even if you request for Bitcoin donations, you do not have to worry about your account being frozen or you being charged with exorbitant fees. You will get more of whatever it is you are trying to acquire. People who want to donate to your cause will be more likely to want to support you as well.

Lower Cost of Transactions

While frozen accounts may be problematic, you need to also be aware of the cost of getting a transaction ready for use. On top of the unexpected risks of frozen accounts and huge chargebacks when you use payment processors, you will also be exposed to well-known high transaction charges for the services of these payment processors. This can considerably reduce the income of your business.

The transaction charges of PayPal, Google Checkout, and Amazon Checkout all begin at 2.9 percent plus $ 0.30 for each transaction. You can enjoy a lower rate of 1.9 percent only if your total transactions for the month amount to more than $ 30,000. Because of this, these exorbitant fees may burden a business with a low-profit margin. The same is true for businesses that require a lot of smaller transactions or those whose products are sold at a nominal price.

The fees that you have to pay when you transact with Bitcoins are all voluntary, and the seller you are transacting with can directly receive those payments. Let us look at an example. If you are an online seller with a 20 percent profit margin, when the transaction fees are eliminated, your profit margin can increase by at least 10 percent since transaction fees are directly deducted from your net income.

In other words, you have the freedom to charge people for sending Bitcoins out and others will have the same freedom when dealing with you. You don't have to spend more than necessary to get a transaction facilitated.

It Works Around the World

The Bitcoin network is considered to be an intrinsically wide-reaching and global network. You will not have to pass through artificial barriers to make payments to vendors who are based in other countries or regions. In fact, it is not quite possible to validate where a particular Bitcoin transaction originated. An online vendor who accepts Bitcoin units as a mode of payment can instantly gain access to a global market with facing the risk of non-payment from customers who reside outside his own country and who are not bound the legal enforcement system of his government.

You should be aware of whether the Bitcoin in your area is valid and viable for use. The legal status of the Bitcoin will vary based on the country you get your transaction in.

Inflationary Hedge for Long Term Savings or Investments

Since newly created Bitcoins have a limit to where only 21 million coins can be created in its lifetime, it is considered to be a good option to store long term value in to provide a hedge against inflationary risks. This is particularly beneficial for those who reside in countries that experience runaway inflation. If you can transfer a big amount of your income into your Bitcoin account, you can be isolated from the increasing rise in the inflation of your native currency. You can simply convert your Bitcoin units back to your native currency when you have to buy goods and services from vendors who do not accept Bitcoins as a mode of payment.

A lot of critics believe that this is still quite early to do this because of the high volatility of Bitcoin prices today. But it is very likely that Bitcoins will soon become a widely accepted currency, which can in turn result to a more stable price. It is already legal in many countries and is on its way towards global acceptance.

Chapter 6

Risks

Bitcoins sound great, but they have their inherent risks. You should be aware of both the benefits and the risks involved before you think of investing.

Irreversible Transactions

As we have mentioned in the previous chapter, vendors no longer have to go through a rigorous process to validate the integrity of their customers because the responsibility now lies with the customers to validate the merchants they will transact with to ensure that the goods or services they paid for with their Bitcoins are reliable. Some of the methods that customers have to go through can seem complicated.

For instance, there are customers who make use of a third-party escrow service to oblige a particular vendor to deposit a performance bond before the client's Bitcoin payment. There are also other instances where both the vendor and the customer may have to take part in an obligatory arbitration of disputes.

The added effort needed to get Bitcoins transferred can be a problem. However, Bitcoins may end up being easier to transfer in the future. This is to ensure that a transaction will move well.

Potential Hacking Threats

Anything in the world of technology can be hacked into if plenty of effort is made and the Bitcoin is no exception to this. One such example comes from how hackers stole about $ 1.2 million in Bitcoins from Inputs.io recently. This came as a result of hacking software designed to find information on the ownership status of Bitcoins. This allowed the hackers to steal the money.

What makes this worse is that the Bitcoin is like cash in that it will be gone without any way to easily replace it if it is stolen. What makes this even worse is that it will be hard for anyone to recoup losses if items are stolen. This creates a strong need to ensure that added protection is used when getting Bitcoins ready.

- Still, people can protect their Bitcoins with a few considerations:
- Consider using an online wallet that is easy to sign up for.
- Transfer any Bitcoins that are earned to an offline device.
- Consider getting an encrypted cloud storage service to work on your account.

If you aren't comfortable about this, then you can always exchange your Bitcoin for the case.

You can do this online or through a Bitcoin ATM depending on where you live and what is available for when you take care of the transaction.

Volatility of Bitcoin Prices

When someone asks you what the value of the Bitcoin units that you own is, how can you readily answer the question? The fundamental value of any particular currency is a function of the consumer demand for that currency and the consumers' capability to use the currency to trade it for valuable goods and services. Because a lot of common currencies are no longer linked to the worth of an underlying product or commodity such as gold and other precious metals, a Bitcoin unit will only be valuable when some people or consumers would want to own them and use them for trade.

The currency experienced a dramatic bubble in the middle part of 2011 before trading caused its value to go down. Today the Bitcoin has a good value attached to it in that 1 Bitcoin equals around $ 2575 USD as of June 2017. Still, the threat of the value of the Bitcoin changing in value is significant.

Currently, there are plenty of public exchanges that have been set up to allow consumers to buy and sell Bitcoin units in exchange for dollars or other common currencies. This aids in establishing a fundamental relative value for Bitcoins that then allow vendors to convert their

Bitcoin holdings into other common currencies on a more regular basis. This minimizes the vendors' risk exposure to the price volatility of Bitcoins.

Even though during the recent years, the price of Bitcoins has greatly fluctuated. There exist methods that vendors can use to quote Bitcoin prices relative to their equivalent value in dollar or other common currency. This also allows them to convert the Bitcoins they have collected into another currency immediately.

Another apprehension about the volatility of Bitcoin prices is that the total amount of all the Bitcoin units that have been mined as of this writing is only a little over $ 14 billion USD. This is based on how 14 million Bitcoins have been mined and also with the value as listed just a bit ago.

This comparatively small market limitation together with the absence of a regulatory body may expose the prices of Bitcoins to become manipulated by the market players. It's like what you would expect out of penny stocks and other items that are not as commonplace; it only takes one or two transactions for the values of certain items to be jacked up and artificially influenced.

There are several important speculations being made in various online forums on who may be behind the price manipulation of Bitcoins and to what extent. It is quite common to hear Bitcoin speculators refer to "The Manipulator" when they discuss significant market movements.

"The Manipulator" refers to an obscure individual or group of individuals that is assumed to be controlling the Bitcoin prices through their vast wealth. But it is not clear as to who these people are.

One thing is for certain that the relatively anonymous nature of the Bitcoin is a huge part of what allows people to adjust the values of Bitcoins as they see fit. This makes for an added risk to the Bitcoin. Of course, whoever is regulating it could always stop doing so and focus on some other kind of investment in the future, but it can be next to impossible to figure out what's going to happen.

Anti-Inflationary

In his article in the New York Times, renowned economist Paul Krugman criticized the anti-inflationary provision of Bitcoin mainly because of the 21 million Bitcoin production limitations. Paul Krugman argued that the production limitation of Bitcoins would trigger people to accumulate the currency instead of spending it.

But I think Paul Krugman's argument disregards the almost never-ending divisibility of Bitcoins. When the value of Bitcoins escalates, it is quite expected that people will still have the desire to spend some of their earnings from their Bitcoin investment by spending a portion of the Bitcoin units that they own.

Unlike conventional currencies that can have artificial inflation through the growing debts of the government, Bitcoins are expected to continue having a comparatively constant value over the long term. A creditor will be very willing to loan some of his or her Bitcoins to other people because he or she can have the assurance that Bitcoins will not go through an artificial inflation before the debtor pays back the money with the corresponding interests.

In contradiction to the argument of Paul Krugman, there are several instances when the deflationary prices in certain industries such as electronics and computers can appear to forecast people abstaining from purchasing consumer products because of an expectation that prices will go down shortly. It is common to hear people saying that they will not spend $ 1,000 on a new computer today because they will rather wait for one to two years so they can get the same unit for less than half the price. Instead, we can observe that a vigorous market can provide an ever-growing value to all consumers.

Of course, all currencies go through inflation, so it will help to be aware of what is open with the Bitcoin. The Bitcoin may not be likely to bear with inflation, but it's a good potential that is worth exploring just to be safe.

Computational Attack

The block chain we discussed in the first chapter is considered as the existing valid or legal ledger of all transactions in the Bitcoin network. It is only possible to extend block chains through a computation intensive cryptographic hashing. Any person or group of persons who wish to illegally re-write the entire history of the block chain will be required to obtain a much superior computational power than the whole population of the Bitcoin network.

When someone attempts to create an alternative history in the block chain, he or she will not be able to create new transactions without the real owners' private keys. But the illegal hackers that work to get Bitcoins can have the capability of erasing old transactions that have already been recorded in the block chain in the past.

In theory, a scammer or a hacker can choose to purchase a product or a service using Bitcoin units. Once they receive the product that they ordered, they can publish an alternative blockchain that is longer than the original one but does not include the scammer's valid transaction. Since the new and illegal block chain is lengthier and therefore proves that it had a stronger computation in the past, Bitcoin network will accept that illegal block chain as the most current and updated version of the block chain.

This loophole in the process permits any scammer to use their Bitcoins to receive goods and services from vendors and to delete the transaction so he or she can own the products that he purchased without have any deductions from his or her Bitcoin balance. This is what is referred to as double spending. It is a process that can be dangerous and harmful to the process of actually getting money to work in some way when getting such a transaction up and running.

It is quite tricky and complicated to accomplish a computational attack in the Bitcoin network today. The totality of the computational power of the entire Bitcoin network now is equal to more than 100 PetaFLOPs. The PetaFLOP refers to the quantity of solved cryptographic puzzles per second.

When compared to the K computer of Japan which is currently considered as the greatest supercomputer in the world today, the K computer is a lot inferior because it has a computational power equivalent to 10.51 PetaFLOPs only. The cost of setting up an enormous supercomputer that will enable a person to hack into the Bitcoin network overshadows any of the prospective gains that can be acquired from the capability to double spend part of the units in the Bitcoin network.

On account of the probable risk of double spending, the Bitcoin network has adopted a new practice of requiring at least six confirmations or six 10-minute blocks to be appended into the block chain before a particular transaction can be considered as valid. Even if an illegal scammer may have the luck and the computational power to invalidate one to two blocks using an alternative chain, he or she will find it harder to completely alter all six blocks because each new block or new cryptographic puzzle becomes more difficult to solve.

Regulatory Ambiguity

The legal category of Bitcoins remains uncertain. Some people consider it as a commodity like gold and silver while other treat it as a viable currency. Still, there are others who look at Bitcoins as a financial product or something that is legally equal to the gold in World of Warcraft. It is yet to be known if Bitcoins will someday require licenses and financial rules and regulations for it to become a truly viable currency. Mt.Gox, which is currently considered as the biggest Bitcoin exchange market, has reported that they have experienced some difficulties in wiring funds because of certain money laundering investigations done by government or regulatory agencies.

But Bitcoins are intrinsically difficult to regulate because no central authority oversees all Bitcoin transactions. As we have previously mentioned, Bitcoin transactions are partially anonymous, and it is quite impossible to freeze a Bitcoin account. Because of these reasons, it is highly probably that Bitcoins can become the primary medium option for people who are into illicit activities such as money laundering and tax evasion.

What makes the Bitcoin market such a concern is that the protected nature of the currency makes it popular among those who engage in illegal or questionable activities. Online users who have a certain level of technical know-how can use the TOR anonymizing network to gain entry to a service referred to as the "Silk Road" which is a trading place for illicit drugs that can be purchased using Bitcoins.

But if we stop and think about it, any paper currency such as the US dollar can also have the same risks as described above. It is also possible to complete illegal transactions anonymously using dollar bills because it is possible to exchange it without any auditable paper trails. But the complexity of the Bitcoin network technology may instigate regulators to see Bitcoins as a hazard to the rules of law.

Be sure to refer to the listing we had not, too long ago about which countries the Bitcoin can be used in. All countries have their standards for how the Bitcoin can be used and the odds are very good that these terms will change well into the future.

Risk of Loss

When you own Bitcoin units, it is quite apparent that you have the responsibility to ensure that your digital wallet is secured from any potential risks of loss and theft. This task or responsibility can be quite taxing, especially if you own a substantial amount of Bitcoins because you will have to use certain tools such as protected encryption, password management, and information backup to make sure that your risks are maintained at a low level.

Several high-profile incidents have already been reported where people made errors and mistakes in handling their Bitcoin accounts, which ultimately led to them losing a big amount of their Bitcoins. Since there is no central authority you can approach to seek help or assistance, you may have to completely write off your losses because they may already be unrecoverable.

The risks associated with Bitcoins are critical and have to be identified. It should not be a surprise that a virtual currency that is relatively new is in danger of being hacked into. You should be cautious when seeing how this currency is run before you make any trades with it.

Chapter 7

Future

The public ledger where Bitcoins are recorded is known as 'Blockchain.' Blockchain is essentially a distributed database that stores records of Bitcoins in 'blocks.' Each 'block' contains a timestamp and a link to the block before. These blocks once set cannot be modified. They are permanent and can be easily verified. Given these features Blockchain technology is highly secure and as a result, very attractive to the financial sector. In fact, in 2014 the Federal Reserve Board, endorsed the use of Blockchain within the industry to make transactions safer; other high profile banks including Goldman Sachs echoed this sentiment.

Many experts believe that Blockchain will disrupt cash and online transactions, with the technology and respective cryptocurrencies underpinning all financial transactions by 2025. Some say that Blockchain will transform payments in the same way that email changed communication.

Blockchain has the potential to reform corrupt systems due to the security it offers. Furthermore, no transaction fees are incurred, compared to present day payment systems, where transaction fees are unavoidable.

Blockchain's potential is not limited to the financial sector. Any form of asset exchange can take place over Blockchain – including instant, secure voting, property sales, books and the distribution of vaccines.

One area where Blockchain technology is truly disruptive is in the insurance space where new models of insurance such as peer-to-peer insurance and micro-insurance can flourish.

Blockchain is moving towards global adoption, and one day it will become what the Internet is now – a system where transactions can be made seamlessly, at zero cost, completely secure and will not be given a second thought.

Conclusion

Bitcoin started out from a paper written in 2008 by a mystery man named Satoshi Nakamoto and is now one of the highest valued currencies in the world.

The story of Bitcoin is both interesting and inspiring. The success of Bitcoin cannot be attributed to just one person but to a collective development. Bitcoin would have never become what is right now if people on Internet forums and investors hadn't worked on developing the software.

Bitcoin has a bright future as more and more countries are looking towards legalizing in it. The value of Bitcoin may be fluctuating, but the returns have mostly been positive for everyone who invested in it. Those who got in early are now millionaires even though they barely spent a few hundred dollars.

The Bitcoin world is huge, and there is a lot you should learn before you step into investing and trading. It's important to research everything before you decide to invest.

Thank you for buying this book AND Please do NOT forget to leave a review so that other are able to see the value added through this book.

Other Titles by the Gary Bukowski

<u>Blockchain: A 60 minute guide to Blockchain Technology</u>

<u>Ethereum: How to make 36 times your money in 1 year</u>

Bibliography/Reference

Original Bitcoin paper by Satoshi Nakamoto: https://Bitcoin.org/Bitcoin.pdf

Bitcoin millionaire list: http://gazettereview.com/2017/05/top-10-richest-Bitcoin-millionaire/

Latest Bitcoin News and Updates: https://Bitcoinmagazine.com/

Bitcoin General Information: http://www.coindesk.com/

Blockchain 101: https://blockgeeks.com/guides/what-is-blockchain-technology/

Current Bitcoin Prices: http://www.coindesk.com/price/

Time of Bitcoin: http://historyofBitcoin.org/

Bitcoin Info: https://Bitcointalk.org/

www.ingramcontent.com/pod-product-compliance
Lightning Source LLC
Chambersburg PA
CBHW050027230526
45470CB00003B/1160